Dedications

For M. and M.

And a special thanks to all of my *Older*

friends who take time out of their day to

share their wisdom and stories with me.

I0491120

Freedom v.s. Comfort

"Those who would give up essential Liberty, to purchase a little temporary Safety, deserve neither Liberty nor Safety."

- Benjamin Franklin

Translation: Those who choose comfort over freedom, deserve neither.

I understand that any form of society has to have rules. Laws that govern behavior

so that society does not destroy itself.
The purpose of those laws is to punish
those who'd harm the members of that
society, but what about when the laws
themselves are worse than the actions
they prevent.

If you like swimming, or taking baths, you
have to risk drowning. Some of those who
drown might even be children. You can be
safe about it, but it still causes a lot of
deaths. I'll be bold and say, water is
necessary, and most sane people would
agree, however swimming isn't and

neither is taking soaking in the tub, or going on a cruise. Yet people have died from all of these, and it would seem absurd to try to ban them. Could you imagine a law that prevents you from doing all of those things ever? Yes, there are laws that make it safer, but when does that safety override one's freedom.

What about alcohol, tobacco, and sugar? They're enjoyable, but far from necessary, and one could easily argue they do more harm than good. If Alcohol was outlawed, there would be no more alcoholics...oh wait. We tried that, didn't we?

During prohibition, everyone didn't stop drinking, and marijuana is heavily in use in the U.S. now in areas legal or illegal. Neither are inherently out to hurt anyone, but when freedom is infringed, it turns those who don't fit their chains into criminals— People who have to drive without insurance, because they can't afford it. People who want to open a small business but can't because of all the regulations, and people who live in a bad area, and want to carry a gun to defend yourself.

Cutting hair, massages, selling alcohol to adults of legal age, having a sanitary hot dog stand are all heavily criminalizing to those who can't jump through the monetary hoops provided, or as some call it, the red tape. Why? People often do these things because they're in a bad situation in the first place. They do it mostly because they have to. It's understandable to get them help, but why make criminals out of them, when it will only make their life will only go downhill even further.

Having to jump through hoops means you don't have rights, you have privileges. Your not a free man, just a very, very, comfortable slave.

There's a classic Aesop fable of a Wolf on the brink of starvation, who runs into a dog. They greet each other as cousins and taking notice of the starving wolf, the dog offers him a job working for his master.

The wolf agrees, but along the way to the master's house, he notices a bald spot on the dog's neck. Concerned, the wolf asks the dog what happened, and the dog replied, that's where his master puts a collar on him so he can't run away.

The wolf says, "Fuck that noise, I'd rather starve. Have a nice day." The moral of the story being— better to [die] free, than be a fat slave. (To be transparent the

I believe America is the best country overall, because of this freedom. It may not best for each individual, but for the most part, even if you don't like an area, you can move to a different place in the state or country (if you have the money.) and most importantly, it's diverse enough for there to be some area to accept you despite where you come from or what race you are, compared to other countries.

I also feel this freedom is becoming more limited each year. We may have fewer shackles than other countries, but that doesn't mean some of the shackles we do have aren't a problem. People are feeling trapped. They are feeling hopeless. With that feeling they become depressed, and seeing no way out they take drastic measures. They do drugs, and they self-harm or harm others. I'll admit I'm no expert, but it appears very clear to me that the answer to so many feeling trapped, is more freedom. Freedom, unfortunately, isn't given, it must be stood up for.

The issue is, people only seem to care when they're young and have don't have

the wisdom or experience to guide them,
or when their long leash finally gets
tugged, and they realize that they should
have made an effort to remove it long ago.
Of course, this is because we are so busy
trying not to stay ahead of current
problems, we don't look at the ones that
aren't bothering us yet. It's when we dash
towards the exit and get yanked back that
we really take notice of the high taxes, the
permits, the fees, the overbearing laws,
the monopolistic businesses, etc.

However, we can do a little every day. Speak up, stand up, and donate, what little you can (after doing your research) to those organizations that support your rights.

Always remember, your first and second amendments are the rights that protect all your others. If you don't exercise them, your rights slowly become privileges. People have fought and died for our rights. Those fights didn't end that long ago, and many are still fighting. What did you do for your freedom today?

Common Gun Misconceptions

1. **The Second Amendment is only for Defense against Civilians.** The most common use of Guns is to either defend yourself or others from criminals who would try and harm you or your livelihood. It then becomes easy to fall into the thought process that the second amendment was made for that purpose. However, it was actually meant as security against a tyrannical

government. It is the main reason our government has never become too overbearing in the first place. If the government ever became out of hand, there are far too many people able to fight back. I believe this is one reason why they've been trying to whittle down the rights because citizens are increasingly frustrated. We could also very quickly deal with any invading force that steps on our land.

However, a not so quick note— I've heard another misconception quite often that fits in this same category.

That citizens could never put up a

fight with a government, because of

the strength of our amazing military.

Two issues with that, Firstly you

don't have to destroy the military to

win, you just have to make them

give up, and there are currently too

many armed citizens and too many

guns to think that'll end smoothly.

Second and more importantly, the

Military is made up of Citizens, so

unless we plan on having a civil war,

I don't think the government would be on the winning side.

I think people who bring up that misconception are thinking of small militant groups, not a mass amount of the population.

2. **Ammo size doesn't matter.** What's better in a handgun, having more bullets or having more powerful bullets? People who prefer having lots of bullets (usually in 9mm/9x19), sometimes are often enough in the mindset that shot placement is the only thing that matters.

Unfortunately, in the heat of a situation, you didn't plan for, bullets aren't always likely to land where you would have hoped. However, with preparation, you have a good chance of hitting who you hoped, but it may not stop the threat fast enough. A more powerful bullet may easily be what makes the difference in how fast your opponent goes down.

3. **Semi-Autos confused with Automatic.** This one of those, chicken little situations. Someone

thinks the sky is falling, and a bunch of people believe it because they heard it from an idiot who lied and didn't bother to look a little further. They then have a problem admitting they're wrong, and the issue spreads. A problem when getting around to voting. A semi-automatic gun is one shot per trigger pull, end of story.

4. **High capacity magazines aren't needed or useful.** Yes, many civilian shootings are handled in the first few shots, however, every

situation is different. Someone who lives in a dangerous area, or has a dangerous job, may fight more than two attackers.

If a person has reason to think someone is out to get them, they may want not only want a lot of ammo but another gun on them as well. Let's also not forget that the gun is for protection against the government too. Do you really think it should be up to Politicians, and the rich people bribing them, to tell you how much ammo you can carry? If the answer is yes, you probably

don't carry, to begin with. If so, go

fix that if you can.

A shooting encounter is not a gun

range. The target moves, they hide,

they fire back. If they really want

you, or someone you love dies,

more than they care about their life,

ten bullets may not be enough

against someone who plotted an

attack out. Laws are universal,

situations are not. So when

someone thinks they don't need a

high capacity magazine, tell them

don't carry one.

5. **911/Police** Many people I meet are

under the impression that the police

have teleportation powers.

Whatever you think of them, I've met

a lot, and don't know any that do.

Yet, there's a lot of people who

think, if anything bad happens,

they'll just call 911, and it'll go away.

This is one of those Wisdom With

Experience situations.

Most of these people have never

had to call 911 in a time-sensitive

emergency, so they don't know how frustrating it can be. Especially in an area where those who respond are spread thin. One of the best things about owning a gun is, you can protect yourself until police arrive. Just make sure your in a situation that demands it, before you use it.

6. **Gun control won't/doesn't criminalize good people.** This one is pretty absurd, but it does get insinuated often by some of those pushing gun control.   They say they are only targeting the bad people—

they only want you to have a license.

They want to make it safe, like cars.

No flight, no fly. They aren't trying to

take away your guns.

Except— Bad people carry

regardless of the law. A license

makes it a privilege, that can be too

easily controlled. You don't need a

license to buy a car, and who people

think is a hate group can be very

political. (Look at all the churches

that get targeted because they don't

approve of gay marriage, or

recognize other religions.)

7. **Silencers make guns very quite**

   They don't, they just prevent you

   from blowing your eardrums out.

   There is no reason you should need

   a special license to own one, let

   alone go to prison over it.

8. **Stand Your Ground and Castle**

   legalize Petty Murder. Using or

   threatening lethal force is a situation

   many people don't find themselves.

   So they, unfortunately, rely on

   outside sources, that only display

   the exceptional, to influence how

   they feel. Unfortunately, that leads

to many misunderstandings. Stand

your ground allows you to defend

yourself from a reasonable threat.

Castle allows you to defend your

home. You would probably do both

if you had to anyway, but the

difference is the aftermath. Without

laws protecting you, it's too common

for those defending themselves to

become the criminals.

9. **Fewer Guns means less suicide.**

In relation to our guns and the

western world in general, The United

States has a very low suicide rate.

Though I feel it could be much lower, guns prevent more deaths than the cause here.

10.   **Gun Violence.** A big issue in the media is the phrase *gun violence* itself. It's often used in a misleading way to

Handguns:

Revolvers VS Semi-Automatic

Quick disclaimer: These are all my opinions, I am not an expert, If you get shot don't blame it on me.

Which is better, a revolver or semi-automatic/autoloader. To me, this is one of the most enjoyable comparisons that are brought up in the "Gun Community". It doesn't take a lot of research to learn the advantages of each type, but because the choice is so personal, the comparison is often made with a lot of bias. What I would like to point out, are situations where I think each would be preferable. These are all my opinions of course, choose what you like and feel safe with, but first allow me to summarize the common advantages of each for self-defense (I'm talking modern guns).

Revolvers

1) The comparable cartridge is a lot more powerful than that of an

autoloader. For example 38 special is a lot more powerful than a comparable .380 ACP, A 357 magnum is more powerful than a 9mm, 44 magnum blows 40 and 10mm cartridges out of the water, etc. Some people skew this fact over bias, but it doesn't take much research to see the truth.

A not so quick note— To those familiar with 357 sig, it is much more powerful than a 9mm, and a .40 caliber but is not more or as powerful as a 357 magnum. Kind of a close but no cigar. The "hottest" 357 sig I've found matches a decent round of 357 magnums and is about 200fps slower than a 357 magnum at it's hottest. They are slightly closer on the lower end of things, but 357 sig gun and ammo are a lot more expensive overall.

2) **Less chance of human or mechanical error.** In the heat of a situation, a lot of things can go wrong. Though guns are now advanced enough that even the cheapest ones have little mechanical

errors, human error is very easy to cause, even with training. Magazine fed guns, that have to be cocked back, with safety removed have a lot of room for issues, where they don't fire when you need them to. Loaded guns without a safety, yes even with well-trained people, have a much greater chance of accidental discharge than a revolver. That's why many agree, a revolver is great for beginners or those who can't afford to shoot extremely often.

3) Eats ammo like a hungry lion.

Sometimes it's not the person or the gun that causes a malfunction, it's the ammo. A lot of Automatic Colt Pistol or ACP cartridges now come in a variety of flavors to fit different wants and needs of the many people who own those pistols. Pistols also vary about as much, if not more, than the ammo does. This results in guns that simply don't shoot every brand of ammo. Since self-defense ammo is expensive, many may not practice with enough rounds to know if that specific ammo is reliable in their gun.

 Not only do revolvers typically not have that problem, even when they do, but it's also a lot less likely to cause a malfunction. (For example, steel ammo may get stuck in the cylinder but the next round will still fire, and you can deal with the stuck round later.)

Also, larger caliber revolvers can almost always shoot a variety of ammo— 357 revolvers can shoot a

.38 special, 38. S&W Long, and short colt.

4) **Heavier trigger pull.** Though there are many hammers fired semi-auto guns with a heavier trigger pull, it generally comes stock in revolvers. This may make you shoot slower but makes it a lot harder to have a misfire.

Semi-Auto

1) **Larger capacity at a comparable size.** Better to have it than not need it, and in cases of multiple attackers, much more useful to have more bullets than a powerful one.

2) **Lighter and thinner at a comparable size.** I lumped these two together because they generally serve the same purpose, which is concealment. If you have to hide a gun on your person all day, it is much better to do so, with a lighter, thinner gun.

3) **Lighter trigger pulls.** Allows for faster follow up shots

4) **Much faster reloads.** Self-explanatory. Magazine fed guns load faster than a revolver, especially for those who are unpracticed in using speed loaders. There is a bit of a catch with this...very few people need to reload in self-defense situations. Still, better to have it and not need it, than need it and not have it.

So, in my personal opinion, what situations demand one or the other?

Well, some thought has to go to why someone is most likely to attack you and a thing sometimes referred to as dead man walking syndrome.

When someone dies from a handgun wound, it's usually because they bleed out eventually. They may not even realize they've been shot until later, and it certainly may not stop them, this is why they're called dead man walking. This is usually solved by two factors. 1. Shot placement or 2. A very powerful round. It's common in the "Gun Community for people to say that handgun rounds aren't very powerful, regardless of caliber. This doesn't really apply to revolver calibers.

If someone is after your car or your body, they may get so close that you'd want to stop the threat with a couple of powerful bullets. Are you in an area with a drug epidemic? The assailant may not feel being shot by a lighter caliber round if he's hyped up on something, or withdrawing so badly he doesn't care, and keep coming after you. In those cases, a powerful caliber revolver may do you a lot more good than a semi-auto.

Also depending on the area, you live in, you may be more likely to get attacked by something on four legs than two. In that case, a revolver in a powerful caliber might also be much more useful.

On the other hand, if you have reason to believe you might be more likely to be targeted, or you're one of those "sheepdog" kind of people, a semi-auto would be much better in my opinion. There is a reason police, and other law enforcement carry it. It's because they are much more likely to face multiple attackers and deal with people expecting them. Good examples would be retail workers/owners, money carriers, or armed security. Also, once again, people with a bit of a "sheepdog" mentality.

People in charge of something valuable,

or who put themselves in danger to protect

others, are more likely to get attacked by

more than one person at a time, and by

someone expecting them to have a gun.

Having a lot of bullets could even be very

useful against someone who is going to

take cover, and keep attacking.

Once again, these are all examples and

just my opinion, carry whatever is legal,

and whatever suits you. If that's the case,

you may be wondering why I even brought

this up. Believe it or not, there is a reason.

Many, as I like to call them: "gun gurus", I've listened to either give little thought to circumstances outside their own. That, or they're such fans of a particular style of gun, that they develop scenarios around what they carry, instead of the other way around. Since most of them carry 9mm G-words, they act as if everything else is secondary, obsolete, or belongs in a dresser by the bed.

For example, once I was in a gun store in Metro Detroit and overheard an old man ask for a pocket revolver because he wanted a gun he could shoot through the pocket of his sweatshirt while he's out and about. His entire outfit was a sweatsuit, so it wasn't like he was going to wear a holster, so it made sense. Personally, I would have suggested a double action only revolver, in 38 special, but the worker just insulted the old man for wanting that in the first place. The employee told the old man to get a certain striker-fire gun that starts with the letter G or "don't get anything at all". The old man thanked him for his advice and left to find a second opinion. Stuff like this happens often.

Another thing I noticed, that I find a little amusing, is people usually start off with bigger guns, and either stop carrying or go smaller. Those who carry long enough to become *gun gurus*, seem to eventually go so small, that they are carrying a gun with the capacity of many revolvers in the comparable caliber. This kills the main advantage of autoloaders, leaving only the weight and concealment factors. The faster reloading is also a factor, but they often stop carrying an extra magazine long before that point anyhow. This removes two significant advantages of autoloaders, which means if you aren't worried about the slightly harder to conceal revolver, and prefer the heavier but safer trigger pull, a revolver seems a clear winner.

There are also people who can't afford certain guns. Especially if they're so poor they have to live in a bad area that demands one in the first place. Gun gurus, often make light of the cost of the decent holster, the class for their license, the bullets for the class, the cost of the license application (which I didn't know was separate when I took it.), the fact that one can get denied after applying for the license and not get that money back, and the bullets for practicing at the range, along with having enough training to not shoot yourself. That could well cost over $1000. THAT'S BEFORE YOU GET THE GUN.

People who get semi-auto's and skimp out on a lot of those steps are much more likely to shoot themselves, than someone with a revolver. That's why they make such good beginner guns, but some people wave that off and tell people to just get a lot of training and you'll be fine with a semi-automatic, when there are a ton of people with training who have shot themselves on accident, because of a cheap or poorly made holster.

As I'm writing this, a decent semi-auto gun will cost a little under $300, add $50 for the price of a revolver with the comparable caliber. Afterward, you can spend a lot less on the other *necessities* accessories, (except for the ammo), and perhaps feel a bit safer with what you're carrying.

Whatever your circumstance may be, do what's best for you. It's a personal choice and once again— I am not an expert, these are just my opinions.

Caliber Wars

For those who aren't too familiar with Gun Jargon— There's a thing known as "Stopping Power", sometimes confused with knock down power. Stopping Power is a vague way to say how effective a cartridge is at stopping someone in their tracks. This can be by death, disablement, or deterring pain.

Bullets, however, shouldn't be confused with cannon balls, though they can sometimes be called that. They pierce, more than they push, so they don't really have "Knock down power". It's like being punched. A punch can knock you down, but it's more due to how you're standing, where you're hit, how badly you were hurt, etc.

So if any bullet can kill, what's the benefit of larger bullets? Well, in a gunfight, people move around a lot, and along with adrenaline factors, they may not even be phased by a small bullet until long after the fight. At least, they don't know they are.

This is why hunters often shoot deers with larger bullets. The death is quicker and more immediate, instead of slow and miserable. Even if you don't expect to kill every attacker, you may at least want them temporarily disabled by the wound or the pain. You know, make them STOP.

Every bullet has its pros and cons, and most people have their favorite few. I'm not an expert, I won't pretend to be, but in my opinion, it's not about what caliber is best, but what's best for you-- despite what some gurus with a bias might tell you. Here are some of the pros and cons of the Most Popular handgun calibers, to make a better decision for yourself, but before that, I feel I should mention something.

.22 long- Revolver and Semi-Auto

Pros:

- Cheap
- Works in the widest variety of guns.
- Light and easy on recoil

Cons:

- Rimfire cartridge, which isn't as reliable, or versatile as centerfire.

- Small and may take a long time for the wound to register or stop an assailant

- Due to its unreliability, it can jam up magazines.

Semi-Auto Rounds

.380 ACP- This is usually considered the bare minimum to use in self-defense. I prefer to go bigger but that's just me. Maybe it's cause I live in Detroit or maybe it's because I'm overcompensating, but regardless the guns in this caliber are often the easiest to conceal, and often loved by those who never like to leave home without a firearm.

The guns are also usually cheap and good for someone who starting out.

- Typical weight from 80 to 90 grain

- Typical velocity from 850 fps low to

  1100 fps hot

- Typical capacity 5 to 8

Pros:

- Low recoil

- Handguns in this caliber are usually

  the easiest to hide

- Guns are usually cheap

- Slides on guns are usually easier to

  manage for people with weaker

  fingers

<u>Cons:</u>

- Small and may take several rounds to get the job done

- Not good for areas where people where thick clothing

- I've noticed many guns in this caliber aren't too accurate, or better put, harder to make accurate.

<u>Stereotype:</u> Better than nothin'

9mm Luger- It's the well-rounded bullet. Can't decide on what's more important in your caliber, weight, speed, or capacity? 9mm is kind of the middle ground for all loads, except I'd say it excels in capacity in most of the guns it's offered in. Like to change things up? The guns are some of the most customizable. It's easy to see why it's the most popular round.

Also, Remember how I said the guns in .380 were cheap, well with 9mm it's the ammo. Since guns in 9mm have become the most popular, ammo is extremely cheap. It's not without its faults, but it's more than enough to stop a bad guy if it hits in the right spots.

- Typical Weight: 115 to 147
- Typical Velocity: 1000fps low to 1300fps hot
- Typical Capacity: 7, 10, 12, 15, 17, 20, 30 rounds (a very wide variety)

Pros:

- Large gun variety

- Guns can be easy to conceal, or if
  not, usually hold a lot of rounds

- Cheap

- Low Recoil

- Most technological advancements
  have gone into this round

Cons:

- Not very big, or fast, and therefore,
  not very powerful

- large capacity is good, but you'll
  probably need it more than you

would with a more powerful, or

larger round.

- Not the best against anything on four

  legs, or anyone taking decent cover

Stereotype: G-word Fanboy/tactical [insert

intelligence insult here]

.40 S&W- This is the middle child of the more popular semi-automatic rounds. It has some love, but not as much as the well-rounded 9mm or the powerful 10mm.

- Typical Weight: 115gr. to 200gr.
- Typical Velocity: 950fps to 1400fps
- Typical Capacity: 10 to 22

Pros:

- Large Capacity

Cons:

- Strong recoil

- Not very powerful

- Guns typically aren't concealable

- Wears guns down fast-harsh on the barrel

Stereotype:

Wannabe Cop (Unless you are a cop,

obviously)/Wanksta

10mm- A large, and very powerful round for a semi-auto. In fact, it's a bit too powerful.

- Typical Weight: 135 grain to 230 grain
- Typical Velocity: 1100 to 1600 fps
- Typical Capacity: 8 to 15 rounds

Pros:

- Big, fast, and powerful for a semi-automatic round.

Cons:

- Heavy recoil
- Wears gun down really, really fast

- Common with criminals (and might be brought up if you're ever in court)

Stereotype: Gangsta

45 ACP- Cartridge fires a big slow bullet, and that's all there is to it.

- Typical Weight: 180 gr., 230gr (common), 300 grain
- Typical Velocity: 830 FPS to 1100 FPS hot
- Typical Capacity: 7 to 15 rounds

Pros:

- It's Big. If someone gets hit, they'll probably notice, right the fuck away.

- Retains speed

- Recoil isn't as bad as some of the slightly smaller rounds

Cons:

- Slow

- Many practical guns in this Caliber have a low capacity for semi-auto

- So wide it penetrates poorly. Can bounce off of hard barriers.

Stereotype: Grandpa/Grandma

Revolver Rounds

Once again, I'm doing the most common Carry rounds, not all revolver rounds. Don't be mad because your .44 special isn't on the list. If it is, you probably know this info anyway.

.38 Special- Easily the most common carry round, guns in this caliber are some of the lightest, and easiest to carry.

- Typical Weights: 110, 125, 130, and 158 grain

- Typical Velocity: 850fps to 1000fps

- Typical Capacity: Five to Six

Pros:

- Light recoil

- Heavy bullet for the size of typical gun

- Powerful for the size of typical gun

- Cheap for a revolver round

- Can be fired in .357 caliber revolvers like it's a fucking BB

- Extremely Accurate (may be the most accurate)

Cons:

- Slow

- Not very piercing

- Guns in this caliber often hold few

  rounds

Stereotype: Comes with a tampon

(Whether that's good or bad, depends on

you.)

.357 Magnum- Very similar in size to the 38 special, yet opposite in performance. Around that comes with a lot of love, and a lot of hate. Why the hate? Semi-auto rounds are a compromised version of revolver rounds and the favorite round of many "gun gurus" is the compromised version of the .357 magnum— The 9mm. For some reason, that seems to ruffle some panties. Not only that, but .357

magnum, shot for shot, generally outdoes most semi-auto handgun calibers in everything except for capacity and recoil. Still has its downsides.

- Typical Weight: 125 (sometimes 130), 158, and 180 gr.
- Typical Velocity: 1250 fps, 1450 fps, to 1700 fps. very hot (yes out of a carry handgun)
- Typical Capacity: 5,6,7,8.

Pros:

- Fast

- Very Piercing, but because of speed, expands fast sending all the force to the assailant

- Guns in this caliber sometimes hold many rounds for a revolver

- Guns in this caliber can shoot 38 special for cheaper practice

- Can be carried in smaller guns, making it easy to conceal

- Large gun variety

Cons:

- Sharp/Snappy Recoil for the size

- Loud As Fuck indoors

- Ammo isn't being advanced with
  technology like semi-auto calibers
  and .38 special

Stereotype: Wannabe Cowboy

44 Magnum- The most powerful handgun round, that's still practical to carry. Made famous by, the movie Dirty Harry. (Even though he might have had a .41)

- Typical Weight: 165, 225, and 240 gr.
- Typical Velocity: 952, to 1400
- Typical Capacity: 6 rounds
  Pros:
  - It's fast
  - It's big
  - It's powerful

- It also fires 44 special

Cons:

- Strong recoil

- only Six rounds

Stereotype: Over Compensating

45 Long Colt: An old, and outdated round, still in production for recreation, and people who like the Taurus Judge, or Smith&Wesson Governor. People who want a big round in a revolver, but don't like a strong recoil may lean towards this cartridge.

On the other hand, there is a bullet called the .454 Casull. It would be the updated version of this, the way .357 magnum is the updated version of .38 special. Unfortunately, though overpenetration is not really a thing to worry about with most handgun rounds (in a sense that they will pass through and continue on to hurt someone else.) .454 does, in fact, have that issue. If someone gets shot with that round, they are going to have a bad day, but so might anyone, or anything behind them. This is why it's not on the list, even though I like the cartridge.

- Typical Weight: 200gr. and 225 gr.
- Typical Velocity: 600 to 1200
- Typical Capacity: 5 or 6

Pros:

- Low recoil for the size of the bullet

- Guns in this caliber can sometimes fire .410 shotgun shells

- It's Big

- Can be fired out of .454 Casull.

Cons:

- Outdated. You might as well get a gun in .45 ACP (They come in revolvers too.)

- Guns are big

- usually, hold few bullets

Stereotype: It sounded cool at the time.

If you didn't see your favorite round on the list, it's probably because it's not that popular. In the case of the .357 sig., it's really just a necked .40 S&W.

Also, there are revolvers that will fire most semi-auto rounds, but they come with the pros and cons of moonclips, and obviously aren't as powerful as their magnum cousins.

Semi-autos that fire revolver rounds, aren't practical to carry, aren't reliable, are extremely expensive, and usually, damage themselves over a very short time.

Once again, I'm not an expert. If I misspoke, please suffer me. This is all just based on what I'm familiar with. I encourage you to do your own research and choose the gun and cartridge that's best for you.

Wisdom v.s. Knowledge

One of the worse things about our society (In the United States), is that we confuse proof of knowledge for proof of wisdom. For example, if someone becomes a lawyer, that generally means they *know* more than the average person about the law. That doesn't mean they make wiser decisions when it comes to laws. A lawyer might still break the law more than the average joe. A better or perhaps more common example might be a doctor who self medicates, with alcohol or prescription drugs. Wisdom, on the other hand, comes with experience and becomes engraved in us over time.

I would rather have the person with years of experience working on my car, than someone who has several certificates, whose only passed a few written tests.

The reason I bring this up? People, especially those in the public eye, read about info, then often give solutions on situations they've never dealt with first hand.

I live near Detroit, and after a few encounters with stray dogs and a raging idiot or two, some of them occurring when I was with my toddler son, I decided I should get a gun. Before I had him, I never felt I needed one, but now I'm protecting more than just myself.

When I went to a local pawn shop, I was terrified. Not because I did anything wrong, and not because of the gun, but I'd heard that if I was denied the background check, I might be arrested and made a felon. Actually, the process went pretty smooth. They called in the Background check, and I made the purchase, but on my way out the door, they had a warning. Drive with the gun in the trunk and the ammo in the front, otherwise, I *could* be arrested and made a felon. Also if I wanted to carry it around, I'd have to open carry until I bought a license.

I talked to a police officer about open carrying and he warned me not to do it. It could make me a target when I walk, and I couldn't drive that way regardless.

So after a class, a lot of money, and an application I had my license. All good right?

Now I had to deal with two more problems. The first being people I know having irrational fears. I won't even call them misconceptions, because it's not that they necessarily believed something, they were just scared of the unfamiliar, which is human nature. Combine that with a few stories they've heard, and they believed my gun might go off at random, that the bullets might just explode in my pocket, or that the only situation I'd need one is one I put myself in. Luckily for those who are a bit older, I was able to dispell some of the fears, but there are some people who just hate guns, or rather that certain people have them which brings me to the second problem— Anti-gunners.

By anti-gunners I mean people who unapologetically hate guns for social or political reasons, despite anything proven to the contrary. Half the time you can't tell if they're lying, or extremely misinformed, but they seem willing to do anything to be proven right so I believe it's they're simply lying. The reason this persists is that so few go through the experience of carrying a gun, they can trick a lot of people who have little use for paying so much to do it legally.

Foreigners who never had guns in their country, young people who can't actually purchase a firearm, people with a medical marijuana card, adults who live on a college campus, and most importantly people who are just too fucking poor, etc., are too concerned with other matters to do proper research on something that's far down on there list of priorities. They're too concerned with trying to keep a roof over their head, they're heat and electricity running, food on their plate, and make something of themselves all at the same time. When you're doing all that, you don't have time to look past the several one-sided news stories that flash in front of them. Let alone speak up against problems that aren't currently affecting their current lifestyles.

People I know, have been murdered,

raped, stabbed and robbed, the vast

majority of them no guns required. It was

because of the area I grew up in. People

were desperate and the laws that

prevented people from doing something

about it. Also, believe it or not, most of the

killers weren't gang members. Fights just

had a way of escalating and eventually,

someone would either get seriously

harmed or killed, even if they just wanted

to walk away, because let's face it, some

people out to get you could easily be a

neighbor, and the police can't always do something about it. It doesn't always have to be over drugs, or territory.

The reason for killing could be jealousy, racism, jealousy, women, jealousy, money, street justice, or jealousy. Not everyone has the same experiences, and that leads us to make assumptions based on what we have seen, heard, and read.

We can also translate those assumptions in a terrible manner. For example, we may hear "Certain crimes are committed by a certain Demographic of people", and translate that to "Most people in that demographic commit that certain crime." Almost all the scammer calls I get are from Eastern Indians or a similar group, that doesn't mean almost all Eastern Indians are scammers. So when we hear "Guns are tools to murder people", we shouldn't translate that to "People only use guns for murder."

For some, guns are a sport, others like to collect them, but most importantly they protect us, and protect our freedom. To solve our issues, we should not silence narratives we disagree with or blame inanimate objects. If we really want solutions, we should observe the problems, and keep asking why.

Thank you for reading.